IN SICKNESS

IN SICKNESS
AND IN HEALTH

A BABY BOOMER'S GUIDE
TO CARING FOR YOUR SPOUSE
DURING A TERMINAL ILLNESS

JOHN C. RAWLINS, JR.

Red Letter Publishing, Austin

In Sickness: A Baby Boomer's Guide to Caring For Your Spouse During a Terminal Illness
Copyright © 2017 by John C. Rawlins, Jr.
All rights reserved.

Book typeset by Kevin Williamson
Cover design by Kevin Williamson

Created in the United States of America

23 22 21 20 19 18 17   1 2 3 4 5

ISBN 978-0-9981714-4-9 (paperback)
ISBN 978-0-9981714-6-3 (e-book)

To my beloved late wife, Sandy,
and our children Bridgett, Angela, and J.R.

ADVANCE PRAISE

"IN SICKNESS is a deeply moving and caring book, and a must-read for anyone whose spouse has been diagnosed with (and is suffering from) a terminal illness. This book underscores the importance of showing one's undying love, commitment, and support through daily acts of kindness, and through the countless little things that we otherwise take for granted before it's too late."

— **LAURA A. WATANABE**
PARTNER, WATANABE LAW FIRM LLC

"IN SICKNESS provides heart advice for tough times. Spoken from his own experience, John Rawlins offers transforming and practical wisdom for living and caring for a spouse in sickness and in health . . . inspiring and impacting the lives of many."

— **PHIL MARSHALL**
PRESIDENT & CEO, HOSPARUS HEALTH

"Such a thoughtful, enlightening guide for the spouse or partner of anyone who is enduring a terminal illness. This book is a wonderful example of what can happen when a true, endearing love dictates your actions."

— **BRIAN HUMBERT**
PRESIDENT, THE MOWER SHOP

"IN SICKNESS exemplifies the reality of cancer patients and their caregivers. Only those who have experienced this dreaded disease appreciate and understand the difficulty it entails. Job well done, John!"

— JOHN ANSON
PRESIDENT, ANSON INDUSTRIES

"IN SICKNESS is a terrific source of loving instruction and personal support for those who find themselves caring for a spouse, or other loved one, with a terminal illness. John's conversational style makes his recommendations readily understandable and refreshingly non-clinical."

— DON NIX
COMMUNITY VOLUNTEER AND RETIRED CPA

"IN SICKNESS is a thoughtful, beautiful meditation on caring for a loved one during a terminal illness. Though I cared for a parent and not a spouse, this book still applied to me and offered wonderful advice for coping, communicating, caring, and connecting in a time of great duress. This book is a must-read for any caregiver facing the loss of a beloved companion."

— HOLLY TAYLOR
PRODUCER, ITV ENTERTAINMENT

ADVICE FOR THE READER

ADVICE FOR THE READER CONTINUED

ADVICE FOR THE READER CONCLUDED

ABOUT THE AUTHOR

John C. Rawlins, Jr., is a speaker, author, and retired executive from the financial services industry. His professional experiences range from taking startups to IPOs or leading revenue generation for a Board of Directors.

Still, John firmly believes his most important work is captured on these pages.

John lives in Louisville, Kentucky, with his fiancée, Kristin Jones. They have six children and ten grandchildren.

Kristin was very encouraging and supportive during the writing of this book.

John feels so blessed to have found Kris and to be able to share the rest of his life with her.

A NOTE FROM THE EDITOR

When beginning work on this book, John made his intentions clear to me: he wished for this book to be open to spouses of all genders. After all, terminal illness can affect anyone.

With the exceptions of his own stories and examples, we agreed to make the text gender-neutral in the following ways:

1. We use "spouse" instead of "husband" or "wife."
2. We use the pronoun "they" instead of "he or she."

Grammarians may argue this is incorrect, and by certain standards they may be right. We justify this decision on two grounds. The first is the inclusion of the singular *they* in *The Washington Post*'s style manual beginning in 2015 (and the reasons they cite there).

The second is the preponderance of this habit in spoken English. For example, the sentence "Anyone should care for their spouse" is more typical in conversation than "Anyone should care for his or her spouse," even if the latter is more correct grammatically.

If we must, we choose conversational over correct.

— K.M.W.

LETTER TO THE READER

On July 3, 2005, my wife's mother, Dottie, was diagnosed with metastatic cancer and given a very short time to live. My family loved her deeply and we were all shattered by the news.

Eight days later, Dottie came home to our house so my wife and her father could care for her. My wife did everything humanly possible to care for her mother; she knew she only had limited time with her and she made the most of it. Dottie passed away 11 days later.

Sandy's father, Robert, a fit 82-year-old, came back to our house to spend some time with us and begin putting his life back together after the funeral. Sandy took care of all of her mother's hospital and funeral arrangements. She was her father's confidante and constant companion here for about two months, until September when he thought it was time to go back home to Rehoboth Beach, Delaware. Sandy drove with him to help sort through her mother's personal items and clothing.

While in Delaware, Sandy started feeling tired and achy. We attributed it to the stress of her mother's passing, to the responsibility of comforting her father, and of course the difficulty of going through Dottie's possessions box by box and drawer by drawer.

Sandy was supposed to be in Rehoboth Beach for 11 days. We talked a couple of times a day, and toward the end of her stay she began to mention that she really wasn't feeling good. I told her that as soon as she got home we would schedule an appointment with her doctor.

The day Sandy was supposed to come home, I received a call from her sister saying she looked very sick and couldn't fasten her pants. What should they do? I called one of our children, a physician, and asked her thoughts. She said to take Sandy to the emergency room immediately.

On September 19, 2005, Sandy was diagnosed with ovarian cancer. Her case presented the way only 10 percent of cases do, with the abdominal area filling with a malignant fluid generated by tumors. The prognosis for her particular cancer was not good. All indicators said she had about two years to live.

Over the next six years, she endured major surgery, multiple chemotherapy sessions, periods of remission, dozens of hospital visits, numerous CT scans, and all other sorts of treatment.

Despite those difficulties, Sandy was fortunate to have a high quality of life for much of that period. Finally, on July 21, 2011, Sandy lost her battle to cancer.

Through all of this Sandy's faith had never wavered. She kept saying that God is trying to tell us something—but what is it? Is there something we should be doing?

In some small way, maybe this book was what I was supposed to do.

Once Sandy was diagnosed, I began to reflect on our wedding vows: *in sickness and in health, for better or for worse.* We'd had the "better" part—we were happily married for 35 years and were very proud of our three children. We'd had the "in health" part: before her diagnosis, Sandy and I had been in good health, as were our children. We had been coasting; it was especially easy to love those vows in the better times.

Suddenly, we found ourselves "in sickness"—and I found that I was completely unprepared, that I had no sense for what the next six years would require. I wasn't ready.

But I realized I must not be alone in this. Surely there are other Baby Boomers who have had to take care of terminally-ill spouses, I thought—but I didn't know where to look, and at first I didn't know what to do. What I realized I could do, aside from loving and tending to my wife, was to write down what I found—to take notes, make observations, and impart the best advice I can for people who walk now through the valley, as I did with Sandy.

May God be with you and your family.

— **John**

1

FORGIVE YOUR FRIENDS

Sometimes, they will say things that just aren't appropriate to your circumstances. They care—they just don't know what to say (or not to say).

For instance, Sandy was out to lunch with three of her good friends one afternoon. Somehow the conversation turned to hair—different styles, different lengths, and so on. Sandy was sitting there with a scarf over her bald head. Did her friends mean to discuss hair in front of her? Of course not. They just forgot.

This will happen throughout your spouse's illness. It's an accident that happens sometimes. Be patient with your friends.

Remember that, to their fortune, your friends are not dealing with a terminal illness right now. Their lives go on; they plan vacations; they live out their lives normally without having to think about what you think about. They will ask how things are going, they will be concerned, they will care, and they will mean it—but they can't understand what you're going through (unless they've been through it already), so they're bound to make some mistakes.

2

BE A LEADER

Your spouse and family are looking to you for strength, direction, and encouragement. It's your charge to lead your family through this difficult time.

It's up to you to give them hope—not a false hope based on nothing, but a constructive hope based on facts that you know at the time.

I would take an improvement in Sandy's CA 125 test (a blood test that measures tumor markers in the bloodstream) and build on the excitement from positive results.

We're winning this battle!
Sandy, the chemo is doing what it's supposed to do!

I wanted my family to know I was doing everything possible to prolong Sandy's life. Still, sometimes I sought out a friend, someone whose wife also had cancer, and we'd cry together. It helped.

You don't have to be perfect, and you don't have to be what you aren't. Just know that you're a leader when you stay by your spouse's side every step of the way.

3

LIVE IN THE NOW

Live for the moment, for today.

It's fun to reminisce about your life before your spouse was diagnosed with a terminal illness, but it's also sad. Some of the memories we would discuss became sharply poignant when I realized that someday I wouldn't be able to share them with the person who created them with me. Sandy realized it too.

So we didn't spend too much time talking about the past.

The future was tomorrow, and next week, and maybe next month, but not much more than that. When you have a terminal disease, your life revolves around doctor's appointments, blood work, scans, chemotherapy and radiation; that's your "work." Even when cancer is in remission, you don't have a lot of time between doctor's appointments and blood work and scans because the progress of the disease must constantly be monitored.

You live in the here and now. Enjoy your life today, right where you are.

4

DON'T TURN DOWN AN OFFER FOR HELP

No matter how strong you think you are, or how in control, thank people who offer you help, and call them later when you actually need help.

As time goes by, you might need someone to talk to about how things are going. If you're in the hospital for a while, you might like it if someone brought you a meal. Maybe someone can help care for your dog while you're away from home more.

Your friends want to help; they just don't know what to do. Enlist their help, especially if they've offered.

5

ALWAYS KEEP SOMETHING TO WRITE ON. LEAVE NOTES SOMETIMES.

Keep Post-it notes, index cards, or some kind of paper in your kitchen, bedroom, and other frequented areas of the house. Aside from jotting down notes, use them to write a quick note of encouragement.

I know we'll get good news today, honey. You have been so brave and you're inspiring all of us. I love you.

Place a note on the table at meal time, or after a shower, or by their side of the bed—anywhere you know they'll find the note.

It's just a small indication that you care and are fully involved with what they're going through.

6

GIVE GIFTS TO YOUR SPOUSE

After a significant event, like the end of a round of chemo-therapy, surgery, or radiation, a little gift can go a long way.

When Sandy finished her first wave of chemotherapy treat-ments, I bought her a diamond pendant necklace with the same number of diamonds as treatments she had received.

My brother Bill and his wife (also named Sandy) sent flowers to Sandy after every chemotherapy treatment she had for almost six years. It meant so much to Sandy because she knew how particular Bill was about sending just the right grouping of flowers.

A gift for your spouse keeps the romance alive, which is so important during her illness. Remember, it doesn't have to be a big purchase; it really is the thought that means the most.

7
STAY POSITIVE!

Look for any sign of hope or encouragement and embrace it. You might not have been a cheerleader, or maybe that's not your personality, but now is the time when you need to be the cheerleader for your spouse. **The most important person in your life needs you!** They need to know that they're going to get through this. You're going to be with them the whole time; they won't be alone.

The underlying issue here is that you don't want your spouse to lose hope. It is up to you, and the other members of your family, to keep her fighting the disease in her heart and mind.

My family was incredible in this way. When I say "family," I mean not only our children, but our sons-in-law and our grandchildren. They knew when Sandy needed a pep talk and when she just wanted to have a normal day. I credit them for contributing to the longer-than-expected life Sandy enjoyed after the diagnosis.

8

BE NORMAL

Lead a normal life, in as many ways as you can, for as long as you can. Your spouse may have a terminal illness, but to paraphrase an expression I've heard, the illness doesn't have your spouse.

Continue to live a normal life as much as you can for as long as you can. The attitude of both you and your spouse is so important, and feeling some semblance of normalcy helps keep the attitude positive.

Don't surrender to the disease! The moment either one of you does, particularly your spouse, the disease wins.

9

CARING FOR YOUR SPOUSE IS YOUR NEW JOB

Whatever your job or position before this life-changing diagnosis, caring for your spouse is now the most important thing in your life.

What do I mean by "caring" for your spouse? What are some of the job description items for this new job?

- Going with your spouse to as many appointments as you possibly can.
- Accompanying your spouse to radiation treatments, chemotherapy, lab work, CT scans, etc. Even if you don't stay the whole time, get them situated and comfortable before leaving. Your spouse needs to know that you're with them, that they're not alone.
- Apply the same vigor that made you successful in your job to your new job, taking care of your spouse.
- Those ideas, problem-solving abilities, and standard procedures you created in your job now need to be applied to the care of your spouse.
- Keep track of the information. Make notes; organize medications, keep track of the symptoms, and chart progress as you go.

10

BE KIND TO EVERYONE AT THE HOSPITAL OR DOCTOR'S OFFICE

This is so important that it bears repeating: *Be kind to everyone at the hospital or doctor's office.*

Face it: you're bound to be unhappy because your spouse is terminally ill. Still, a lot of the medical professionals you might encounter have to deal with the terminally ill every day, too. They might not be real happy about that part either.

Over the course of dealing with a terminally ill patient like your spouse, the entire medical staff becomes invested in your spouse's care, too. They have emotions and feelings about your spouse and their circumstances too. Be nice, stay calm, and be thankful.

Go to the trouble to thank people for helping with your spouse. This group should include not only doctors and nurses, but aides, technicians, administrators, food service personnel, and so on.

You want them to take good care of your spouse. Be sure you take care of them.

11

LEARN PEOPLE'S NAMES AND RESPONSIBILITIES

Everyone likes to hear their name, and they have more ownership of your problem or request when you address them by name.

Find out who does what—it will make it easier when you need something.

Learn who's on what shift, and from when to when. Make notes on it and keep the notes with you. However modest, information is power!

12

LEARN WHERE THINGS ARE KEPT IN THE HOSPITAL

It takes a long time for staff to bring things, especially non-essential items, if the hospital is busy. Where do they keep extra towels, washcloths, blankets, cups? Where's the ice machine, water, snacks, and other services?

Don't be helpless and wait for everything you need. When your spouse is cold and needs a blanket, get up and get it.

Usually, the hospital staff won't mind small things like this because they're busy too, and they'll appreciate your initiative helping them help your spouse.

13
DEVELOP A TIMELINE

Develop a timeline of everything that has happened during your spouse's care and treatment. This should include a chronology of all tests, major treatments, lab work, and other results. It's very useful to keep this timeline handy in your folder of information.

Keeping a daily journal will make the timeline much easier to see. Written entries will prevent you from sitting there and guessing when certain things happened. Your doctor will want details as specific as you can provide them, and a daily journal will help you provide them.

It's your spouse—be actively involved in their care.

14

MAKE A FOLDER WITH YOUR SPOUSE'S COMPREHENSIVE MEDICAL HISTORY

This is a file of all documents, office visits, hospital stays, lab results, and other paperwork since the initial diagnosis. The folder should contain notes on treatments, observations, reactions to medication and treatments, and information like the timeline I suggested you develop on the previous page.

This file should have your personal notes from office visits, but it should also include notes from anyone you've talked to regarding your spouse's treatment and health, whether during a specific appointment or not. Document your questions for the doctor, then document the answers.

Ask the hospital(s), doctor(s), and treatment centers for copies of reports, lab results, and any other hard information you haven't received already—everything that involves your spouse.

The medical professionals—especially the ones downstream who need the information for treatment—will appreciate your organization and involvement.

Take this file with you everywhere.

15

WRITE OUT YOUR QUESTIONS FOR THE DOCTOR

Doctor _____

Today's Date: _____

- Greatly appreciate all you have done

- Clarify where we are regarding CA 125, neuropathy
  and side effects

- CA 125
  — Dr. _____, score of 40 on March 2
  — Dr. _____, score of 25 on March 13
  — IV Taxol and carboplatin administered on March 14th
  — Could the CA 125 be below 25 now?
  — If not below 25, could it be below 35?
  — What is the number we want right now?
  — Is it reasonable to check her CA 125 and see where it is?

- Side effects
  — Nausea
  — Itchy

- Neuropathy
  — Tingling, burning, itching hands and feet
  — Sleep deprivation

16

MAKE AN ISSUES CHART

Make an Issues Chart. Include the date, time, issue or symptom, resolution, and additional comments.

The reason to do this is to track everything of significance that happens to your spouse between appointments, treatments, lab tests, and so on. When you want to discuss specific patterns, this is what gives you useful information.

Take this with you to your doctor's appointments.

17

MAKE A HOSPITAL PACKING LIST

If you are going to the hospital on a frequent basis, you might want to have a list of things you will need each time you go. It saves you the time and hassle of remembering everything your spouse (and you) want to be comfortable. For example:

PACKING LIST

- Feather pillows in plastic bag (three-day stay, extra pillowcases)
- Tea bags
- Oatmeal
- Slippers
- Clorox® Wipes
- Blue footies
- Glasses
- Personal wipes
- Robe
- Computer, cell phone, iPad
- Long sleeve gown
- Bed jacket
- Cosmetic bag
- Bible, books, magazines
- Devotional book
- Music
- Prescriptions, pain pills

18

MAKE A LIST OF YOUR SPOUSE'S MEDICINES

Make a list of all medicines your spouse is taking and take it with you to all appointments.

MEDICINE	DOSAGE	NOTES
Betapace AF 80mg	½	Every 12 hours
Zofran 8mg	1	Every 8 hours for nausea
Tamoxifen 20mg	1	Daily
Lexapro 20mg	1	Daily
Fosamax 70mg	1	Weekly
Phenergan 25mg suppository	1	Every 8 hours if needed for nausea
Aspirin 81mg	1	Daily
Calcium w/ Vitamin D, 500mg	1	Daily

19

MAKE A DAILY MEDICINE CHART

DATE	TIME	MEDICINE	DOSAGE	TIME GIVEN	NOTES
		Oxycodone 5mg	1		Can give 2 if needed
		Betapace AF 80mg	1		Every 12 hours
		Lexapro 20mg	1		Daily
		Oxycodone 5mg	1		
		Zofran 8mg	1		8 hours for nausea
		Mag-Oxide 400mg	2		Every 8 hours
		Oxycodone 5mg	1		
		Oxycodone 5mg	1		
		Zofran 8mg	1		Every 8 hours for nausea
		Mag-Oxide 400mg	2		
		Xanax 0.25mg	1		Daily
		Betapace AF 80mg	1		Every 12 hours
		Oxycodone 5mg	1		
		Oxycodone 5mg	1		
		Zofran 8mg	1		Every 8 hours for nausea
		Mag-Oxide 400mg	2		Every 8 hours
		Phenergan 25mg	1		If needed for nausea
		Phenergan 25mg	1		If needed for nausea
		Miralax 17grams	1		Constipation
	Midnight	Dexamethasone 4mg	5		Steroids (pre-chemo)
		Neupogen 300mcg	1		
		Emend 125mg	1		Pre-cisplatin
		Emend 80mg	1		Post-cisplatin
		Emend 80mg	1		Post-cisplatin
		Dexamethasone 4mg	2		Post-cisplatin

AM   **Temperature**   _____

PM   **Temperature**   _____

20

USE DISINFECTANT WIPES

Take some wipes to the hospital and wipe off everything your spouse is going to touch. Bleach wipes like Clorox® Wipes are very handy for this task.

Wipe off everything you expect him or her to touch: the telephone, TV remote, bed control, nurse's station remote, side bars on the bed, table by the bed, movable bed tray, toilet seat, sink knobs, door handles, and so on. Be thorough.

It's no bad reflection upon the hospital staff; there are germs and infection in hospitals and you're just taking the right extra precautions. It is more an expression of your love and devotion than anything.

21

ALWAYS TAKE THESE DOCUMENTS WITH YOU TO THE HOSPITAL OR MEDICAL FACILITY

- Durable Power of Attorney for Health Care (make copies)
- Living Will (make copies)
- List of medicines
- Insurance/Medicare cards

22

CONSIDER GIVING A GIFT TO THE HOSPITAL STAFF

If you were pleased with how they treated your spouse, send the staff flowers, chocolates, or a big cookie after you've left the hospital. People remember that kind of thoughtfulness.

When you return, you're a friend coming back and they remember you. It's all about keeping your spouse comfortable and well-treated.

23

KISS YOUR SPOUSE

Kiss your spouse! I don't mean a prudent peck on the cheek like you're going to catch something. Don't kiss her like you would kiss your grandmother. Whether it's your husband or your wife, kiss them like you did the first time you knew you were in love, a real kiss like you did when you first got married.

Nothing has changed in the way you feel about each other; your spouse just has an illness. Make sure that your spouse knows you love them in everything you say and do. It is very important that they know they are loved.

This is the person you fell deeply in love with many years ago. It's easy to do the "in health" part of your wedding vows; the "in sickness" part is much more difficult.

They need to know that you love them now more than ever.

Remember, the disease is not contagious; don't ever treat them like you think it is.

24

HOLD YOUR SPOUSE'S HAND

Hold your spouse's hand. Touch them, hold their hands, and hug them often. The human touch means so much in the healing process.

The human touch is so nurturing. Hold each other. As before, as always, this is the most important person to you in the world.

25

I LOVE YOU

What a powerful, wonderful, honest, sincere—yet simple—thing to say.

I love you.

Say it often. Your spouse needs to hear it.

26

LITTLE THINGS MEAN A LOT

When your spouse is feeling better, don't think that you need to do something "big." An overseas trip or a long vacation might not be their idea of relaxation, especially not if the trip isn't important to them or if it could sap their strength. Enjoying home and family might feel more important.

On the other hand: if they love to travel and want to take the trip, it might be good. This is about what they value and enjoy doing, right?

27

KEEP ROMANCE IN YOUR LIFE

Keep the same spark that you had before! Send flowers, write cards, gifts. Your spouse is still the person that you fell in love with and wanted to be with for the rest of your life.

It is very important that you continue to do the romantic things you always did for them. If anything, take it up another level.

28

KEEP A SENSE OF HUMOR

This may not seem like the time for it, but you need a sense of humor. If you don't have one, you'd better get one, and quickly!

One day, Sandy and I were sitting in an examining room waiting for the results of a CA125 test. (This test measures tumor activity for ovarian cancer patients.)

We had a feeling the news was not going to be good. So we waited, and waited, and waited...

I put my hand under my chair and my fingers touched something sticky. I got up and washed my hands in the sink, and as I was drying my hands off, I looked directly at my wife and said, mocking a doctor's-office drone: "What brings you to the office today?"

We both laughed and it helped ease the tension and fear.

A sense of humor can defuse a lot of situations.

29

PRAY WITH YOUR SPOUSE

Pray with your spouse. It does help. Ask friends and loved ones to pray about your spouse's illness.

Pray about appointments, lab tests, scans, treatments, hospital stays, all the things that worry you.

Sandy was a member of a woman's group that prayed each week for her to have the strength to face her illness.

Many doctors we encountered believed in the power of prayer.

30

EMBRACE YOUR SPOUSE'S LIFESTYLE

Be part of what they're doing or interested in. It doesn't matter if you didn't enjoy certain things that you did together in the past. Things have changed and now it's about spending precious time with the one you fell in love with years ago.

After Sandy's diagnosis, I became an *American Idol* fan and an avid watcher of *Dancing with the Stars*. Not all at once, mind you; before Sandy was diagnosed, I would have been washing my car (or even watching the grass grow) instead. But the illness of your spouse can change quite a bit about you.

In many cases we get smarter about what really matters in life. I know I did.

31

LEARN HOW TO USE A NEEDLE.
YOU CAN DO IT!

If at some point during your spouse's illness you return to the doctor's office to have a weekly shot administered, ask if you could do it at home. In some cases, you can get a prescription and keep the needles at home. You're not trying to replace the doctors; all you're trying to do is make your spouse comfortable.

Just think: one less trip to the doctor's office, meaning one less round of pains and inconveniences. Instead, one quick trip to the refrigerator and you're done.

Giving your spouse a shot can be a very touching way to show you care.

I was the son of a doctor and one of my children is a doctor, but I had no idea if I could give my wife a shot in the arm myself. *Would I pass out or get sick?* Guess what—I did fine. I'm sure you will too.

Sometimes, when I needed to give her a shot and she had company, I would walk through the room on my way to get the needle and say to Sandy, "Please remove everything from the waist up. I need to give you a shot." Everyone would laugh and it would ease some tension in the room.

There's that humor thing again.

32

NOTHING IS OFF LIMITS

Nothing is off limits. You will do anything to keep your spouse feeling better.

You will help them bathe, put on lotion, use a portable toilet, change a dressing—whatever it might be. We might shy away from offering these forms of help, but it will bother you far less than you expect. In the end, there is nothing you won't do to make them feel better.

II's all about caring for your spouse. You will have a chance to learn things together.

Sandy, for example, had a gastrostomy tube that had to be flushed out routinely. Did I have prior experience doing this? No—but I could learn. The nurse showed us what to do in the office and we were able to do it ourselves afterwards.

The flushing of this gastrostomy tube became a source of some pretty funny exchanges.

33

SOMETIMES CARDS AREN'T FUNNY

Sometimes cards aren't funny, touching, or helpful. Sometimes they're depressing. Depending on how the day is going, a card can be upsetting.

We had just returned from an oncology appointment and Sandy's CA125 was up, which meant she would have to begin chemotherapy again. As I looked through the mail, I handed Sandy her cards.

One of the cards was the type of card you send someone who has a cold or the flu, and not a terminal illness like Sandy's. It was signed, but with no personal note; it gave the impression that the person had simply checked off a box without any real caring. Send Sandy a card—check. She was upset that they just didn't seem to sympathize with what was happening in her life. Be there to listen and console.

34

NOT EVERY DAY IS GOING TO BE A GOOD DAY

That sounds obvious, doesn't it? But like the title of this book, the point is that, in the equation of good days and bad days, you can't pretend the tough parts don't exist.

There will be some days when your spouse will not want to look on the bright side. They have a terminal illness with which they cannot argue. Likewise, there will be some days when it won't feel okay, and you will have to listen and sometimes not try to make her feel better.

One day, in the fourth year of Sandy's almost six-year battle with cancer, she wanted to see the timeline of her illness to date. She wanted to know how many months had passed between when the cancer was in remission and when she'd had to start chemotherapy again. Unfortunately, the length of time her cancer was in remission was getting shorter. It was a very sad afternoon and I couldn't do much to change things or help her feel better. I felt helpless and very sad.

If your spouse is continually depressed, talk about it and agree to talk to your physician about their depressed feelings during the next appointment.

One final note, without minimizing anything I've written: sometimes a nap can make all the difference.

35

RESPECT YOUR SPOUSE'S DIGNITY

When giving a shot or changing a dressing—when a private area might be exposed to you—use a towel, sheet, or spare garment to cover that area.

It was something I noticed about one of my wife's doctors: how kind he was about never leaving her exposed during any type of exam. He would always move her gown as he examined her so she never felt like she was laying there without any clothes. She felt he was very protective of her dignity.

Your spouse will appreciate your respectfulness.

36

PICK THE RIGHT DOCTOR— YOU'LL BE TOGETHER A LONG TIME

With a terminal illness, there will likely be one doctor who directs your care regimen and to whom you return regularly. Spend some time talking to people in your circumstance and ask who treated them. Talk to the doctor; if there's a fit, you'll know it. If not, keep looking.

Whether or not you expect it, your doctor will become part of your family.

Sandy had unwavering faith and trust in her oncologist. Sandy would have done anything he asked her to do. I credit him and his good practice of medicine for the almost-six years she had rather than the initial diagnosis of two years.

Choosing the right doctor is the single most important decision you'll make concerning your spouse's care.

37

ADVICE FOR OFFICE VISITS

Get involved, but don't get in the way.

There is a certain flow to most procedures or office visits. Observe it and learn it; it'll help you know what to expect in the future. The sequence is usually (A) receptionist, followed by (B) technician, then (C) any physician's assistants (PAs) and finally (D) the doctor.

The doctor and staff will usually do lab tests; they might also check weight, check their blood work, and review recent changes in medication and outlook since the last visit.

Don't be afraid to ask questions. If anything, have a list of questions prepared, along with the reason you're asking.

38

DON'T ANSWER FOR YOUR SPOUSE

Don't answer for your spouse unless they are unable to (or want you to).

You might find yourself in the examining room with your spouse and their medical team, and it's natural that you can't help contributing. It's fully understandable; you're very concerned and want to make sure all questions are answered thoroughly.

You're trying to make things easier for her. But your spouse has a terminal illness; that likely doesn't mean they became completely dependent upon you overnight.

Your spouse wants to answer the questions about their issues and symptoms themselves. Your spouse is the authority on themself.

If there is something you want to add, defer to your spouse. Try placing it after something like, "Honey, could I add to what you said?" By doing so, you're asking your spouse's permission and acknowledging that it's ultimately their call to make.

39

YOUR SPOUSE WANTS TO BE IN CHARGE OF THEIR OWN HEALTH DECISIONS

There will be times when you wish your spouse would do something and they won't. Leave the room nicely, take a deep breath, and remind yourself: it isn't your body or your decision. Respect that.

For example, some alternative medical practices may be appealing and promising to you, and you may want your spouse to try them. Trying them has to be their decision, not yours. Support their decision, whatever it is, and don't keep bringing it up every chance you get.

40

BE CAREFUL INVESTIGATING YOUR SPOUSE'S ILLNESS ON THE INTERNET

You might not want to know everything there is to know about your spouse's illness. The Internet is full of hypochondriacs.

There are some reputable sources, but you'll start reading, and before you know it, you'll be reading about bad prognoses and you'll become distraught.

Remember, you are the positive force here! If you need reputable information, ask your doctor—who knows your situation and about the direction the care is taking.

Believe in your healthcare team and what they are doing.

41
GET FIT AND STAY FIT

You're going to need to be in tip-top shape.

You're a caregiver, and you'll be called upon to do many different things that your current lifestyle might not include. For example, you could offer to wake in the middle of the night to make sure medicine is administered every four hours. Aside from unpredictable tasks like that, you'll be busy with the tasks you already know to expect: going back and forth to the hospital, doctor's offices, scanning centers, and so on. The time won't just take a toll on your spouse; it will also take its toll on you. Make sure you protect your own health so you'll always be there to answer the call.

As I wrote before in number 4, don't turn down an offer for help—ask for help from friends or family if you need a break, even just a nap.

Exercise is a great stress reliever and keeps you in shape to care for your spouse. However empathetic you may be, be careful not to slip into atrophy or inactivity; it doesn't help either of you for you to lose your strength.

At least, don't get too comfortable with the comfort food. I did and I gained weight (more than I should have).

42

ADVICE FOR THE CAREGIVER

Find a friend or a support group with experience helping a loved one through a terminal illness and talk with them on a regular basis.

I have a friend whose wife was battling a terminal illness before Sandy was diagnosed. After Sandy was diagnosed with ovarian cancer, my friend and I would meet a couple of times a month, and we talked on the phone regularly. It just helped to talk with someone going through the same thing I was.

43
IT'S OK TO CRY

It's OK to cry. Make sure your spouse knows that, and make sure to remind yourself of it.

There will be times when the emotions and circumstances are overwhelming. Crying lets both of you open up more to each other in this hard moment. You really will feel better after a good cry.

44
GIVE YOUR SPOUSE SPACE

This is a tough one. How much attention should you give your spouse? There are times when they will want you sitting by the bed holding their hand. Other times, they will need their space.

It doesn't mean they love you any less; it just means they want to be alone. Don't smother.

45
YOU'RE THE GATEKEEPER

There will be days when your spouse does not want any phone calls or visitors. It doesn't mean they don't like them anymore; it just means today is not a good day for them. Don't be judgmental; your job is to manage the flow of people for your spouse and to protect them when they don't feel like talking or visiting.

Respect your spouse's wishes about visitors or phone calls.

I took this role very seriously; sometimes Sandy would have to remind me: "Be nice to my friend when you tell them not to come over today." I always tried to be nice, but I was very protective.

46

LEARN TO USE THE LAUNDRY ROOM

If you don't already know how to do the wash, learn your way around the laundry room—what soaps, softeners, bleaches, and other chemicals to use and when. Which of their clothes go in the dryer, and which ones get hung up to dry?

Stereotypically, this advice applies more to men caring for their wives. Even if you're a man and you can already do laundry, be aware that garment care can be different for women's garments if you're not used to laundering them yourself. Learn how she does it so you can do it.

By the way: if you're not doing so already, you will be washing not only your spouse's clothes, but all of the house linens: bath towels, sheets, kitchen towels, and so on. You'll also be making the bed(s) and folding and putting away those clothes; you're taking over these responsibilities completely.

Remember that laundry, like so many other tasks, isn't just a chore; it's a way to provide comfort to your spouse. For example, a fresh nightgown for a stay at the hospital is much more comfortable, as are fresh sheets at home. It's all about their comfort.

47

SETTLE INTO YOUR KITCHEN

Get comfortable in your kitchen. You should be able to make at least five basic dinners that your spouse enjoys, or meals they'll like during the treatments.

There might be an occasion when your spouse does not want the hospital food and you will want to be able to fix one of their favorite meals and bring it to the hospital. Then, when they are home, you will be able to make them dinner.

Don't forget lunch and breakfast. What is their favorite cereal and how do they like their eggs? What lunches do they enjoy?

What is their favorite snack?

48

YOU'RE THE DESIGNATED SPOKESPERSON

Your friends will want to know what's going on with your spouse's health and treatment. It is important to have a clear, consistent message for everyone. If you have people who are "tapped in," ask them to call friends and family with updates when you provide them. CaringBridge.org is one very helpful tool for providing updates to friends and family.

Sometimes you might want to update everyone yourself, but repeating the same information over and over again can wear you out. Call your spokesperson or spokespeople and ask them to call others for you.

Friends will be happy to help out.

49

THINK OUTSIDE YOUR COMFORT ZONE

Water the plants.

Decorate for different seasons and for the holidays (if your spouse will be home). If nothing else, you can bring some decorations to the hospital room.

Send flowers.

Send cards.

50

BRING YOUR SPOUSE'S PILLOW

Take your spouse's personal pillow to the hospital. They will appreciate that and it will feel good—certainly better than the hospital's pillow.

51

CHANGE YOUR SPOUSE'S SHEETS OFTEN

Change your spouse's sheets often, and especially their pillow cases and gowns or pajamas.

Again, it's all about their comfort. Nothing feels better than fresh sheets!

52

BE MINDFUL OF HAIR

Your doctor may tell you that hair loss is a possibility with the treatment your spouse is undergoing. Once their hair starts to fall out, consider buying some clippers and cutting all of the hair off. Otherwise, large sections of hair can come out at night during sleep, or they can end up on the floor of the shower. If that happens, it's a sad and depressing sight. By clipping it off in advance, you are trying to lessen the impact of losing their hair.

We had some clippers that I'd used to cut my son's hair when he was little. The first time Sandy began to lose her hair, she asked me to find the clippers and clip her hair off. I got a stool and a sheet to use, like a barber would, and asked her: "How would you like your hair cut today?"

Hers was a very personal decision and I know that. All I'm saying is that shaving Sandy's head worked for her.

If your spouse decides they want to shave their head, as Sandy did, go out and buy some scarfs, wigs, or hats.

If your spouse doesn't want their head shaved, that's fine too. There are no right or wrong answers, just personal preference.

53
BE PREPARED FOR ANGER

- Why me?
- Talk to your spouse about the feelings they are having, about the anger that is inside of them. You will have this discussion numerous times over the course of their illness.
- There is no right answer or justification.
- Be prepared for your own anger and feelings of unfairness. It is a natural stage of the grieving process, one that begins before she is gone.
- You just need to hold her and talk about it, cry about it, and pray about it.

54
GET DRESSED UP

Sandy never went anywhere without looking nice. She did her makeup, styled her hair (or a pretty scarf when she had no hair), and put on stylish clothes. I know that her appearance, and how she felt about herself, helped her keep a positive attitude about her disease.

At Sandy's visitation, I had a woman come up to me and say, "You don't know me, but your wife and I had chemotherapy together. I was sitting in the office in sweats, my hair was a mess, and I had no make-up on. Sandy encouraged me to dress up, do my hair, and put on make-up whenever I went anywhere. I did and it always made me feel better. I will always be thankful for her advice."

55
THINK ABOUT QUALITY OF LIFE

You may have heard this expression from friends or the medical community. But do you know what it actually means? It means that, at some point in your spouse's battle with their terminal illness, you will both have to make a decision. This might be the most important decision you will ever make in your life.

You will be deciding together that you have fought this illness for a long time and you have had successes—periods when the disease went in remission.

However, you might have reached a point where the days they feel well are less numerous than the days they don't feel well. It is now a quality-of-life question.

Wouldn't she rather feel good for a month than feel good only four days a month for six months? That was the sort of decision we reached.

Your spouse might want to live as long as possible for a certain occasion, like the birth or graduation of a grandchild. They might not be as concerned about their own quality of life during that time.

These are tough questions that you and your spouse will have to discuss. Once you reach a decision, talk to your doctor and they will help you choose a course of action based on your spouse's wishes.

A month of good days allows your spouse to see children, grandchildren, great-grandchildren, and friends—in a way more likely to help your spouse feel pretty good when visiting with them.

The decision about quality of life towards the end can be the greatest gift you and your spouse give to one another.

56

BUY A BURIAL PLOT (OR PLOTS)

It's very difficult, when your spouse is feeling good, to raise the subject of looking at burial plots. It's even more difficult when your spouse is sick. However, she might have strong feelings about where she wants to be buried or if she wants to be cremated.

Have these discussions early. Make these decisions together.

I did not do this and my family and I were forced to make some decisions without my wife's involvement. I wish she could have been involved with this decision.

57

SELECT PICTURES OF YOUR SPOUSE

Spend some time reviewing pictures of your spouse with family and friends. This gives your spouse an opportunity to exercise some control over the pictures that people will be looking at. It can be a very tender time as you review your life in pictures. This also eliminates your having to rush through pictures before a memorial service.

I missed this one. I wish Sandy could have helped me choose the pictures we used. As it was our children picked the pictures out and did an excellent job. But I still wondered what pictures we missed that she might have wanted included.

58

KNOW YOUR SPOUSE'S FAVORITES

- Bible verses
- Hymns
- Praise songs
- Radio/TV preachers
- Songs
- Movies
- Television shows

59

CONSIDER HOSPICE OR HOSPARUS

I can't say enough about the exceptional job that Hosparus did in the final stages of Sandy's life. They are the most caring, committed, knowledgeable people on the planet. What they do on a daily basis is a blessing for a terminally ill spouse.

The staff at Hosparus will meet with your family and discuss what course of action they plan on taking to help your spouse through this final stage.

Hosparus will come to your home on a schedule to which you all agree, based on their experience with the stage of your spouse's illness. At first, it might be every other day, just to check vital signs. It might be for other tasks like bathing your spouse.

When anyone from Hosparus came to our house, it was as though they were a longtime trusted friend. I felt a great sense of peace after they became involved; Sandy's long battle with cancer was coming to an end, and she would be pain-free and able to visit with her family and friends.

When the time has come, don't hesitate to get them involved. In our case—I contacted them after we made the decision to take a break from chemotherapy. We realized the chemotherapy could no longer hold back the progress of the cancer and her body couldn't take any more chemotherapy treatments.

60

THE END OF LIFE

You've brought in Hosparus.

If you haven't talked about the end of life by now, it's time.

Burial or cremation ceremony, church or funeral home—all of those options need to be discussed.

I have a friend who believes, "When it's over, it's over," that funerals are ultimately for the living. But if your spouse has any special requests, now is the time to find out.

61

RELIEVE ALL PAIN YOU CAN

With the advances of modern medicine, there is no reason why your spouse should ever have to deal with pain. Don't wait and hope they feel better; call your doctor and say you need pain medication for them.

During your next doctor's appointment, review your spouse's symptoms and tell the doctor about any pain.

62

ACCOUNT FOR JEWELRY AND OTHER PERSONAL ITEMS

Once Hosparus has been brought in—or before this, even—your spouse should consider going through any jewelry or personal items and determine which items your children or relatives should receive. This allows your spouse to visit with family members and give the items to them personally. It can be a very special time as your spouse shares each article—its history, their time with it, and why they're choosing to give it to the person they are.

After Sandy and I made the decision to bring in Hosparus, we talked about who should get different pieces of jewelry. It was so important for her to determine who got what and why. This eliminated me having to guess, or our children having to go through a very difficult process sorting that out without her input.

Sandy was able to visit with each one of our children and give them the items that she wanted them to have. It was a very loving and touching time for everyone.

63

MAKE FINAL ARRANGEMENTS

Hosparus will encourage you to make a decision on what funeral home will be handling your spouse's service. Do this in advance, because everything will move very quickly once your spouse passes away and this is one important decision you will want to have made already.

Sandy passed away around 2 a.m. and I immediately called our children and Hosparus. Hosparus sent a nurse to our home to confirm that my wife had passed away and complete the Certificate of Death.

My children with their spouses began arriving and were able to see their mother one last time. I then called the funeral home and asked them to come pick up Sandy.

64

LET YOURSELF RECOVER

You will have a hole in your heart and feel more sadness than you can imagine. But you have diligently worked to make your spouse more comfortable, to love and honor them, to be their health advocate, to support their every need through this grueling process; you have earned the right to mourn your loss, knowing that they always felt loved.

Over time you will begin to heal and your life will slowly become normal again. But it will be a new normal.

The blessing for both you and your family is that you all gave the caring of your terminally ill spouse everything you had in you. Don't spend time second-guessing yourself; they would not want you to do that.

You honored your wedding vows—*in sickness and in health.*

May God bless you for the way you cared for your spouse.

A GRATEFUL FAREWELL

Caring for a terminally ill person comes to a conclusion at some point. You know this from the beginning of your walk together.

I cared for Sandy for almost six years during her illness, and it is here that I memorialize my thoughts and suggestions from that time. It is my earnest hope that sharing these experiences will prove useful to you, and more, that they might make you feel less alone in your struggle.

While I am deeply saddened that Sandy is gone, my over-whelming feeling is gratitude. I am grateful for my time with Sandy, including every day during the six years of her illness.

My final advice: stay positive, live in the now, pray together. Love your spouse.

Everything will be all right.

www.ingramcontent.com/pod-product-compliance
Lightning Source LLC
Chambersburg PA
CBHW030301030426
42336CB00009B/478